A DOGFACE'S WAR

A DOGFACE'S WAR

◆

A Paratrooper's Story of WWII in the Philippines

Edward W. Hogan

God Bless !

Ed Hogan

iUniverse, Inc.
New York Lincoln Shanghai

A DOGFACE'S WAR
A Paratrooper's Story of WWII in the Philippines

Copyright © 2007 by Edward W. Hogan

iUniverse books may be ordered through booksellers or by contacting:

iUniverse
2021 Pine Lake Road, Suite 100
Lincoln, NE 68512
www.iuniverse.com
1-800-Authors (1-800-288-4677)

ISBN: 978-0-595-42904-2 (pbk)
ISBN: 978-0-595-87241-1 (ebk)

Printed in the United States of America

This book is dedicated to my best friend:
Mary Eileen Hogan

Contents

History of the 511ᵗʰ Parachute Infantry Regiment

By: Leo Kocher

The 511th PIR (Parachute Infantry Regiment) was activated at Camp Toccoa, Georgia on January 5, 1943, under the command of LTC Orin D. Haugen. He was promoted to a full Colonel a few months later. The cadre of the 511th PIR were selected mainly from the 505th PIR which was then stationed in Fort Benning, GA. The Regiment was formed from about 12,000 recruits, of which about 3,000 were selected to start basic training. From the latter number around 2,000 troopers formed the Regiment, of which 173 were commissioned and three were warrant officers.

On March 23, 1943, the 511th PIR closed at Camp Mackall, NC to join the 11th Airborne Division, under the command of Major General Joseph M. Swing. Following 17 weeks of basic training, the 511th journeyed to the Fort Benning Parachute School for three weeks of jump training. It should be noted, with all the extensive training, no 511th PIR soldier who boarded a C-47 refused to make the jump.

In December of 1943, the 511th returned to Camp Mackall for Advanced Training. The success of the Knollwood Maneuvers was very instrumental in the continued use of Airborne troops during the remainder of World War II. In January of 1944, the Regiment departed Camp Mackall for Camp Polk, Louisiana to engage in further maneuvers and prepare for overseas movement.

In April of 1944 the 511th departed Camp Polk for Camp Stoneman, California. On May 8, 1944, the 511th PIR departed from Pittsburgh, CA on the SS Sea Pike with about 2,000 troopers that had been disguised as a "Straight Leg" infantry unit. The ship had been built by the Western Pipe and Steel Corp. and launched in Feb. 1943. The ship was 492 feet long, with a beam of 70 feet. She drew 29 feet of water and her steam engines pushed her at 17 knots. On May 28, 1944 the Regiment arrived at Oro Bay, New Guinea.

While the 511th was in Strategic Reserve in New Guinea (May–October 1944), they conducted Airborne, Jungle and Amphibious training. On Nov. 7,

1944 the Regiment departed New Guinea by ship (USS Cavalier) for the Leyte Campaign in the Philippines. From November 18 to December 27 the Regiment participated in the Leyte Campaign in the Abuyog, Dulag, Burauen, Anonang, Manaraawat, Lubi, Mohonag and Anas areas.

The 511th went into reserve in the Dulag area from Dec. 27th to January 21, 1945. From Jan. 22 to Feb. 2, the Regiment prepared for the forthcoming jump on Tagaytay Ridge and moved to Mindoro by sea and air. On the 3rd of Feb., the 511th jumped on Tagaytay Ridge, Luzon. From there the Regiment moved to the Paranaque and the Pasay area and fought in the Ft. McKinley and Alabang area until Feb. 19, 1945. On Feb. 11, 1945 Col. Orin D. Haugen (the Regimental Commander) was mortally wounded and died of wounds on Feb. 22, 1945. Lt. Col. Edward Lahti, the 3rd Battallion commander assumed command and remained in command until August 1947.

On Feb. 23, 1945, in an effort to rescue the many prisoners (2,147) still under Japanese control at the Los Bonas prison, B-511th, plus the light machine gun platoon from HQ1, made a dawn jump on the prison at 0700 hours. Together with a simultaneous attack, by a Reconnaissance Platoon and Filipino guerrillas, the prison was captured. Amtracks (amphibious vehicles from the 672nd Amphibious Tractor Battalion) were used to transport the prisoners to safety. The plan envisioned the immediate evacuation of all prisoners and military personnel to the security of the Manila area. It was almost a textbook operation, no fatalities were suffered on the entire mission and all prisoners were rescued.

The Regiment fought in the Real, Mt. Bijiang and Santo Tomas areas from March 4 to March 24, 1945. From March 24 to April 11, 1945, the Regiment less the 3rd Battalion, operated in the Bauen and Batangas areas as 6th Army reserve. During this period, the 3rd Battalion was attached to the 188th PG and fought in the Sulac, Sapac, Talisay and Malaraya Hill areas. From April 12 to May 4, 1945 the 511th fought in the Lipa and Mt. Malepunyo area. In May 1945, base camp was set up near Lipa, Luzon. On June 23, 1945 the 1st Battalion and Companies G and I, boarded troop transports, from the 317th Troop Carrier Group, at Lipa Airstrip and dropped by parachute near Aparri as part of the Gypsy Task Force. The 511th PIR sustained a total of 289 killed and/or missing in action causalities during the Leyte and Luzon Campaigns.

On August 11, 1945 the Regiment departed Luzon by air and was flown to Okinawa. On August 30, 1945 the 511th arrived by air, at Atsugi Air Base near Yokohama to occupy the city and guard the docks from which the peace delegation left to go to the USS Missouri and the signing of the Armistice. On Sept. 16, 1945 the 511th moved to Morioka, Japan to begin the occupation of Iwate and

Aomori Prefectures in Northern Honshu. Separate companies were stationed from South Morioka, all the way north of Honshu to the city of Aomori. In January of 1947 the scattered units started to move in to Camp Haugen near Hatchinohe. In February 1947, Regimental Headquarters moved from Morioka to Camp Haugen. During the months of January through March of 1947, the Regiment was brought back up to T/O strength.

1

In January 1943, World War II was in full swing and patriotism was at fever pitch. My two older brothers and most other friends my age were already in uniform. My brother Jim was headed for the Navy V-12 program in Philadelphia while Bob was at Great Lakes Naval Training Station in Chicago going through basic training. To get into the service at this time, it was necessary to go through one's respective draft board. Two friends and I wanted to get into the Marine paratroopers but it just happened that all three of us belonged to different draft boards. We each went to our designated draft board and asked to be drafted on the same day. It was a good plan but alas doomed to failure. I went in to the Army on February 26, 1943, Rene Verlinde to the Army Air Corps one day later and Jack Allen into the Marines two weeks later. (The Marines Corps' monthly quota apparently had been met before the middle of February, but had not been met in March when Jack Allen made his choice.)

On that fateful morning I awoke with the tune "This is the Army", from the show of the same name, reverberating in my mind. How appropriate for that day. After breakfast and having said good-bye to my mother, brothers Dick, Dan and Tim, and sisters Mary Frances, Barbara, Betty Jo and Trisha, I climbed into my Dad's 1941 Hudson for the drive to the Michigan Central depot on Vernor Highway near Michigan and 14th. Inside this busy "crossroads" (normal traffic plus at least a couple hundred inductees) I was surprised to see my Aunt Frances McCarthy, affectionately known as Aunt Zaz. After saying good-bye to my dad and aunt, I passed through the gate anxiously awaiting my first train ride and a future of ever changing incredible events.

Ft. Custer, near Battle Creek, was an induction center. Inductees were given their uniforms, inoculations, and IQ tests and most were on their way to another camp after three days. Recruits, with one exception, were not given a choice of which branch of the Army (Air Corps, Infantry, Artillery, etc.) they would serve in. Selections were based on physical conditions, IQ and need. The one exception to avoid this selection process was to volunteer for the paratroops. This is what I did so after about a week, while the army collected enough paratroop volunteers to fill a troop train, we were on our way to Camp Toccoa, Georgia.

This small army camp, in the red clay country of northeast Georgia, was set up to screen paratroop volunteers and form units that would then be ready to start basic training. The 501st and 511th Parachute Infantry Regiments were then being formed. As a matter of fact, the 1st and 2nd Battalion of the 511th had already been constituted and had started basic training in Camp Mackall, North Carolina.

The first test the recruits had to pass was the jump off the 35 foot mock-up tower. Candidates put on a parachute harness whose riser strap was hooked to a cable about 35 feet off the ground. The cable sloped gradually toward the ground where at the lowest point it was about 10 feet off the ground. The idea was to jump off the tower and fall free for about 10 or 12 feet before the fall was arrested by the harness/cable setup. From there you slid down the cable to ground level. The rookies found out that 35 feet off the ground is a long way! Most passed but some did not.

Another test was climbing Curahee Mountain, not really high as mountains go but steep, and for these out of condition rookies, a real test.

The flimsy barracks in Camp Toccoa each had a small pot belly stove. It was of course impossible to keep a fire going all night without constant attention as naturally the fires would go out. One learned quickly that sleeping on a cot with no mattress and only two blankets, one blanket had to go underneath the sleeper and one on top.

The last test was a stiff physical, then an appearance, naked, before the brass. All in all about 50 percent of the volunteers were rejected and sent to other outfits. The "lucky" ones soon boarded a train for Camp Mackall, North Carolina. I was now a member of the 1st squad, 1st platoon, H Company, 3rd Battalion of the 511th, 11th Airborne Division.

Private Ed Hogan, 1943

At this point, a cadre had been selected for the regiment, consisting of all the officers and most of the NCO's (non-commissioned officers). They had come from other Airborne Divisions, mostly the 82nd, who prior to shipping overseas were stationed at nearby Ft. Bragg. (Two guys in our platoon had brothers in the 82nd Airborne, which distinguished itself in jumps in Sicily, D-Day in France and others.)

2

Camp Mackall was in the sand hills area of south central North Carolina, about 60 miles east of Charlotte. It was a new camp built quickly after the start of World War II. Although adequate, the barracks were sparse. As soon as we got there intensive basic training began. This included close order drills, firing on the rifle, machine gun, submachine gun and pistol ranges, and lectures on a wide variety of subjects. Daily calisthenics and double time running three to five miles at a crack at irregular intervals was also included.

Ed Hogan in front of barracks, Camp Mackall, N.C. 1943

We also learned how to take apart and put back together the various weapons, how to dig a foxhole, put up a pup tent and of course, do KP (kitchen police).

In the first part of June we boarded a train for Ft. Benning, Georgia where three intense weeks of jump school awaited us. We settled in the "Frying Pan" area of this large camp, an area well named because it is the hottest place I have ever lived in. I can still remember eating lunch in the mess hall and having the perspiration roll off.

The first week of jump school was devoted to "conditioning", jumping off the 35 foot mock-up tower and learning how to tumble when you hit the ground after jumping off a four foot platform.

The second week we learned how to pack our own parachute and "jump" off a 250 foot tower. Actually, you put the harness on with the chute already deployed and were raised up 250 feet and then released. The tower had four long arms at the top but only three were used on any given day because of the wind. (It wouldn't be any fun being blown into the tower.)

On Monday of the third week we rode over to the airfield in trucks and boarded planes for our first jump. I was excited and nervous because this would be my first flight in an airplane. Normally training and combat jumps are made at the 600 to 800 foot level. However, these first few were made at 1200 feet apparently to give these rookies a somewhat better and longer view of the land-scape.

Paratroops boarding transport plane, Camp Mackall, N.C.

The hook was attached to a 15 foot strap which in turn was tied to the top of the parachute. The hook was fastened on a cable running the length of the plane near the ceiling. As the plane took off, nervousness abounded and much perspiration, not related to atmospheric conditions, developed (known as sweating out a jump). As we approached the jump zone, the command "Stand up and hook up" was given followed by the command to check the chute of the man in front of you. After checking, the confirmation was hollered out "Number 12 OK", then "Number 11 OK" and so on down the line. When the plane got over the jump zone the green light came on and the jumpmaster (who didn't jump) patted the man standing in the doorway on the back of the leg and yelled "Go". Out went the first man followed by the rest. Jumping technique called for a trooper, as he jumped out the door (which was on the left side of the plane), to kick his right leg out and make a quarter turn to the left, thus facing the rear of the plane. As he fell, the 15 foot strap hooked to the cable inside the plane became unraveled, which then pulled the parachute out of the pack. When all the way out, the string tying the chute to the strap broke. The blast from the propeller then filled the chute, which caused a sudden shock. Occasionally the risor straps on the chute brushed against the back of the neck causing "risor burns". It was a great relief when a trooper's chute opened and he realized he had passed his first major hurdle. The view was incredible but it didn't take long for another realization: one had to land safely and this was by no means guaranteed! Degree of landing difficulty depended on atmospheric conditions, especially the wind. After landing and gathering his chute, the trooper headed for a waiting truck for the ride back to the hangar.

This was a time of great exhilaration. Everyone had a story to tell. How close they came to another jumper on the way down, what their landing was like, etc. It was, to be sure, a feeling of great accomplishment!

We made a jump every day that week so that after the Friday jump we had qualified for our paratrooper wings. That evening I was anxious to call my parents who had been led to believe (without lying) that our five jumps would not occur until the following week. Shortly thereafter we boarded trains for the trip back to Camp Mackall and some in depth training.

Back at Camp Mackall as July, 1943 began it was time to get into some more advanced training. These next two months, July and August, turned out to be the two most miserable months of my life up to that time. We were on a five and one-half day week—Monday through Friday were training days while Saturday mornings until noon were for inspection of personnel and barracks. Every weekday after breakfast, we fell out into formation then marched out Range Road anywhere from three to six miles. Once out in the sandy, scrub pine countryside of North Carolina, we worked on squad, platoon and company "problems", how to take advantage of cover and concealment, how to dig a foxhole, etc.

The Battalion mess hall sent lunch out to us but the gnats by the thousands made eating a trying experience. They loved to buzz around the face and ears nearly driving one nuts.

The march back to camp in the late afternoon summer heat was no picnic either. Standard uniform at that time was army fatigues, with long sleeves of course, and each man had a backpack, cartridge belt, etc. In the rifle squads the standard weapon was the M1 rifle for everyone except the machine gun team who shared the duties of carrying the 30 pound machine gun and 12 pound tripod. (The machine gunner and assistant were assigned an M1 rifle and carbine, respectively, but these weapons were not carried on most training exercises.) The M1 rifle weighed about nine pounds and the carbine about five.

Occasionally we would encounter threatening weather during our marches back to camp. In such cases, one of the guys would holler "Send her down Davey—big drops and close together!" I don't know where this saying originated but if the rain did come it was welcome. Nothing like a good rain to cool you off!

At Fort Benning we had learned the basics of parachute jumping. Now it was time to learn the intricacies: how to assemble after a jump, how to recover the supply bundle (which was pushed out of the plane in its own chute), how to make a night jump, etc.

Parachute jumping was relatively safe but occasionally an accident would occur. On our first night jump one of the guys had a "streamer" (where the chute does not open completely). He was killed. More common were sprains or breaks in the ankle or leg.

A big regimental night jump was scheduled near the end of the summer where the planes would fly out over the Atlantic Ocean, then return, simulating an invasion. The drop was to be made near Florence, South Carolina an area completely foreign to us. We were taken to the air field in trucks and waited … and waited. There was a bad storm in the area and the jump at the last minute was postponed. Psychologically, this was bad for the troopers. Sweating out a jump was always the worst part of it. In this case we had to go back to the barracks and start out all over again the next day.

After a jump most of the guys had the same feeling of exhilaration. As a matter of fact, many expressed a desire to go right back up and make another jump. However due to the shortage of planes and pilots, jumps tended to be infrequent. On average, we jumped about once a month but sometimes it was two or three months between jumps and the longer the period between jumps the worse the "sweating".

The jump at Florence, S.C. was successfully made the following night. After going through the prescribed training exercise and bivouacking there a couple nights we were flown back to Camp Mackall. This flight was the first time I actually landed in a plane after taking off eight previous times and parachuting out! Another recollection I have of this flight is our company commander, Pat McGinnis, dropping a beer bottle on a farm house as we flew over. He missed! (We always flew with the plane door open.)

Another hurdle we had to overcome to become qualified infantry men was the 25 mile march. As noted earlier, the 1st and 2nd battalions had been formed prior to the 3rd, consequently they were way ahead of us in training. In order to catch up it was necessary to take short cuts. One such short cut was to schedule a platoon jump followed by a live ammunition exercise on the same day we were to go on the 25 mile march. The jump was made pretty much without incident after which we assembled at the appointed location. We then moved out and attacked the enemy. During this part of the exercise our platoon leader, 1st Lt. Bob Kitz (from Toledo) almost had a coronary as he feared we were going to shoot each other. This didn't happen and we were soon on our way back to camp, part of the way in trucks (the Army again showing it is all heart!).

That evening somewhere around 9:00 or 10:00 p.m. we started on our 25 mile march. A few interesting things occurred during the march. One was that we learned this necessity: to conserve water. Each man had his own canteen but there were no water stops during the march. Another was the unusual event of a man falling asleep while marching. This happened to the man in front of me, Bernard Denich, from Chicago. He would start drifting off to the side of the road and I would shake him before he fell into the ditch. About 7:00 or 8:00 a.m. the next morning, we arrived at the Ft. Bragg Military Reservation where we set up pup tents, dug latrines and otherwise prepared for our week long stay. One incident from this stay I'll never forget was one afternoon we were moving across this field and the machine gun team, including me, was lagging behind. Second Lt. Oliver, a favorite of General Swing's because of his polo playing skills, hollered at us to catch up. We eventually did the machine gun and tripod notwithstanding!!

When it was time to return to Camp Mackall, the brass decided the machine guns would return by truck. This was a big break. We left around 8:00 p.m. and were back in camp around 4:00 or 5:00 a.m.

3

Going home was never very far from the average GI's mind. During the summer of 1943 the Division policy on furloughs was announced. Basically, 15 to 20 men at a time would be allowed to go on two week furloughs with the dates for each decided by lottery. Big smiles and loud groans (depending on what date you got) greeted the announcements as most of the guys were anxious to get home for the first time.

My first furlough was in October and that meant I had to borrow a suitcase. That wasn't hard thanks to the generosity of one of my comrades in arms. When the day to leave arrived we took a bus into town (Southern Pines if my memory is correct), then boarded a train for Washington D.C. There we changed trains and after a short layover, boarded a New York Central train for Detroit.

I wanted to surprise my parents so I hadn't advised them of the exact date I would be home. After arriving at Michigan Central Depot, I grabbed a Checker Cab and headed for the East Side of Detroit. While driving down Mack Avenue, I noticed my brothers Dick and Dan and a friend, John "Fatbutt" Odor, standing in front of the Polar Bear Ice Cream Parlor. I had the taxi driver stop and I got out and joined my brothers and friend.

Ed Hogan (in uniform) brother Dick (third from right) and friends goof-ing around in front of the Polar Bear Ice Cream parlor, Detroit, Michigan, 1943

The three of them walked into the living room first, where my mother and dad were entertaining another couple. My mother started to yell at them for using the front door but she stopped when she saw me. It was the longest separation from my parents so far, easily exceeding the 2 two-week stays at Camp Ozanam, a Catholic youth camp. This was the first time I entered the house at 3645 Chatsworth, as my family had moved after I entered the Army. The big joke was they moved but I found out their new location.

Ed Hogan in yard of home on Chatsworth, Detroit, 1943

4

About this time in Washington D.C., a big argument was going on as to whether an entire airborne division could be successfully landed behind enemy lines. In an attempt to answer this question, the 11th Airborne Division was ordered to land the entire division in a training exercise in North Carolina in December 1943. Present for this occasion was the Secretary of War, Henry Stimson, as well as a number of Army brass. Involved in this display were the 511th Infantry, 457th Field Artillery paratroopers, the 187th and 188th Glider Infantry as well as other divisional units. The exercise was a huge success, so much so that the Army decided to activate additional airborne divisions.

Our tour of duty at Camp Mackall ended in early January, 1944. We boarded trains for Camp Polk, Louisiana, a large camp in the southwestern part of the state. This was a permanent camp as opposed to a wartime, temporary camp which Mackall was. The barracks were much nicer. They were two stories with separate rooms for the Non-Commissioned Officers (NCO's). This area of Louisiana had swamps which was our first clue that we might be headed for the Pacific area. The camp also contained a large prisoner of war (POW) section. We often wondered what the German POW's thought while they were playing soccer inside their compound when they saw our formations go double timing past them. The war was over for them for sure. By all accounts, the German POWs were treated well in the United States.

Our training there was relatively routine except for near the end when we went on maneuvers for several days. Our defensive line and foxholes were examined with a fine tooth comb—everything had to be just right.

We made one jump while at Camp Polk. It was not one to practice assembling the company after the jump or to attack a presumed enemy—it was just a simple jump, probably to remind us of what our role in the war was and keep us sharp.

A few weeks before we left Camp Polk, things became very tight and rigid. There were no more weekend passes or furloughs. One detail I was on was putting a special grease on the battalion pots and pans then baking them in the oven. This was done to prevent rust in the steaming jungles of the Pacific.

One day in April 1944 we boarded trains for Camp Stoneman, adjacent to Pittsburg, California (up the bay from San Francisco). It was of course my first trip in the west and the mountainous scenery was absolutely amazing. Occasionally our train had to sit on a siding for an hour or two waiting for another train from the opposite direction to pass.

The scenery at Camp Stoneman was very impressive. There were six feet deep irrigation ditches among the rolling hills and everything was green, green, green. It was at this camp that I first heard that famous platoon cadence song, "Sound Off" from a platoon of black troops.

After a few days at this camp we boarded trucks for a trip to the wharf where the ship, the S.S. Sea Pike, awaited our regiment. The C3 cargo ship built by the Western Pipe and Steel Corp. was nearly 500 feet long with a beam of 70 feet. The S.S. Sea Pike held approximately 2,000 paratroopers, disguised as "straight leg" infantry. (Later we learned why we were disguised. When two men from H Company happened by General Douglas MacArthur's headquarters on Leyte Island, they were greeted cordially and invited in. They asked him why the 511th didn't get any publicity or recognition for their battles on Leyte and he replied that he didn't want the enemy to know he had an airborne division in reserve.)

To board the ship we had to walk under a portal at the top of which was the sign "THROUGH THESE PORTALS PASS THE BEST DAMN SOLDIERS IN THE WORLD." It was an inspiring sign. We were assigned a bunk below deck. Bunks were 5 high and were back to back with very narrow aisles.

Passing under the Golden Gate Bridge was a real downer. Cars and buses traversing the bridge were very visible and the occupants of these vehicles of course had easy access to coffee, donuts, etc. at the closest coffee shop or restaurant. It didn't take a rocket scientist to figure that this was just one of a long list of deprivations and inconveniences we would be subjected to for the foreseeable future. We had already been told that we would only get two meals a day on ship, breakfast and dinner.

On the afternoon of the first day out, those of us on deck got to view one of the most incredible sights I had ever seen. A school of porpoises, probably about a dozen glided in and out of the water together, with utmost grace. Those in the know said these incredible sea animals were aware the ship was close at hand and were putting on a show for the passengers and crew. Some show!

Aboard the S.S. Sea Pike, 1944

Other than this incident, the crossing was relatively boring. After the first few days, we were in a warmer climate and some of the guys chose to sleep on the steel deck. When we crossed the equator a rather elaborate initiation took place on deck where a few representative members of the regiment were given "special treatment". Many others were doused with a fire hose. I was now a pollywog and was numbered among the many Trusty Shellbacks. This was definitely official because it was approved by Davey Jones and Neptunes Rex.

5

After a couple weeks we pulled into Milne Bay, New Guinea to pick up a pilot for the final stage of the voyage to the Buna/Gona area. (Another "metropolis" in the area was Dobadura.) Horseshoe shaped Milne Bay was my first view of the beautiful tropics. The land rose rather steeply from the water's edge sometimes at an angle of 45 degrees or higher with trees and dark green jungle growth everywhere. At various levels there were small hutments and in the evening the lights from the hutments presented a tranquil sight. It was a far cry from the Detroit River back home.

After 16 days, the S.S. Sea Pike dropped anchor at our destination, Oro Bay, New Guinea. We had to climb down rope ladders to waiting landing crafts. We also had to load our duffle bags by lowering them via rope. I was picked to relieve one of the men doing this and the first one I handled slipped off the hook into the Pacific Ocean! It happened to be my buddy Dick Ostrom's but fortunately it was recovered, although most of the contents had to be hung out to dry. The landing craft took us to the beach where we debarked.

We boarded Army 6x6 trucks and were driven inland about 5 miles to our new camp. Pyramid tents had already been set up in long rows. Across from H Company's a row of tents was I Company and back to back to them was the rest of I Company. Beyond the last row was the baseball field and beyond that, fields of kunai grass which grow to six or seven feet.

Behind our camp, some distance away were the Owen Stanley Mountains which have to be the ugliest mountains in the world. They were positively eerie. A good part of the time the peaks were covered with fog or clouds.

All the enlisted men's tents were on one side of the regimental road while battalion mess halls, officers' quarters and mess halls, and "theatre" were on the other side. The theatre consisted of a screen; a guy sat on the ground or brought his own device to sit on. The mess hall consisted of a kitchen and a covered area with several long counters about chest high which were the "dining tables" (you ate standing up!).

Our training in this area continued. There were jungles nearby so we were quickly acclimated to the southwest Pacific area. Very close to the camp, an air strip was built using steel matting which was very common in WWII where an

15

airfield did not exist. During the six months or so we were in New Guinea we only made one practice jump and of course the planes used this air strip.

Probably the most popular recreational activity was the "theatre" where movies were shown several nights a week. (I still remember the song "Long Ago and Far Away" from one of the movies.) Of course the theatre was outdoors and the only thing covered was the projector. It was always a good idea to bring your poncho in case of rain. The movie "Rhapsody in Blue" featuring Gershwin music, is one that was viewed (on Leyte) even though a steady rain persisted through most of the movie.

Another favorite pastime of many of the guys was swimming although because we were still on a five and one half day "work week" this activity was confined mostly to Saturdays and Sundays. We were fortunate to be only a couple miles from a narrow river flowing from the Owen Stanley Mountains which featured clean water and a depth of about 12 feet. On one side was a cliff, gradually rising to a height of about 25 feet. It was therefore possible to climb this cliff and dive from different heights. Another advantage of this swimming hole was a first class diving board built by some other Army outfit. To get to this spot we always hitchhiked and it was usually easy to get a ride from various army vehicles. There was no civilian traffic, the area being occupied by natives with whom we had trouble communicating because of language differences. Transportation was one of the main reasons we seldom went to the ocean to swim. It was much further and more difficult to catch a vehicle going straight to the beach.

Ed Hogan and Dick Gayhart, New Guinea, 1944

Six man touch football was another popular sport. A strong rivalry developed between our first platoon team and the third platoon team. Unfortunately one of our sergeants took over our team (of course he had bet on us) and some of the guys didn't play much if at all. I was a starting end. Maybe it served him right—we lost a close game.

On October 20, 1944 U.S. Army forces invaded Leyte Island in the Philippines. Ships that landed one of the divisions came back to New Guinea to pick us up. Our ship, the U.S.S. Cavalier, was a Coast Guard ship with what we considered a great chef and great food. A rumor widely circulated was that the 11th Airborne Division Commander, General Swing, told the ship's captain that he had shrunk his men's stomachs while on New Guinea and he wanted to keep them that way. Therefore, he should feed them sparingly and with the same kind of food they were used to (canned beef, Spam, dehydrated potatoes, powdered eggs, etc.). The Coast Guard Captain told General Swing that while they were on his ship he would feed them the same food he served his own men. The food was truly delicious including items such as pork chops which we had not seen on New Guinea.

The voyage to Leyte took about 7 days and we had no sooner dropped anchor when the air raid alarm sounded. Fortunately the all clear sounded before any enemy planes appeared. We climbed down rope ladders into landing craft for the trip to the beach. Our first assignment was to help unload the ships which because it was the rainy season on Leyte was kind of messy. However dreary a job like this may have been it did have one advantage. When the situation was right a case or two of canned fruit cocktail, peaches, etc. would disappear into the weeds to be recovered after dark.

After about a week on the beach the first platoon was ordered to assemble for a special announcement. The platoon was commanded by two officers: platoon leader and assistant, (first and second lieutenant, respectively). Next in line of command was the platoon sergeant who of course was an enlisted man. In this situation one would expect the announcement would be made by one of the officers, presumably the platoon leader. However, our Platoon Sergeant, Buford Atkinson, affectionately known as "Sergeant At", had been with us since Camp Toccoa (the officers had not) and had a very strong presence. Whatever the reasons it was obvious that on this Saturday evening Sergeant At was going to speak to the assembled group. He got our attention then said very dramatically: "Monday morning we replace the 7th Infantry Division in combat!" One could hear the proverbial pin drop but in truth it should not have been a surprise for after all we had been in training for over a year and a half for this day. Nonetheless it was a somber thought, for each of us knew that for some death could be just over the horizon … and it was.

Monday morning came and went without us going into combat for reasons not divulged to us lowly "dogfaces" (a nickname for infantry men). It was Thanksgiving week and late Friday we were given a big piece of cold turkey. That was the extent of our Thanksgiving feast (but our motto was be thankful for the little things). It was announced that our trek into the Leyte Mountains would begin the next morning.

Our jumping off point was near a village where most of the Filipinos did not speak English. It was here that we witnessed women doing their laundry: dunking the clothes in a stream, beating them with a stick, dunking them again then ringing them out. The last task was to brush their teeth with their index finger.

Before we departed I gave my canteen to a young Filipino boy, probably about 9 or 10, to fill with water. When he didn't come back right away, I went looking for him and found him after a short search. He thought I had given him the canteen as a gift! Not recovering the canteen would have been an unmitigated disaster.

The load we carried going into the Leyte Mountains was greater than any we experienced during training. In addition to all the "camping" equipment, each man had nine boxes of K rations, enough for three days. Every rifleman had 8 clips of M1 ammunition in his cartridge belt (8 rounds to the clip) plus 2 bandeliers of 6 clips each across his shoulders and two hand grenades. There were 4 boxes of machine gun ammunition (250 rounds per box) in each 12 mm rifle squad. The assistant machine gunner had the responsibility of carrying the 30 pound machine gun (he also had a 5 pound carbine) but the only way a unit could be successful was to share the load.

Little did we know when we started the march that we would not see another vehicle until we had crossed the mountains and reached the west side of Leyte. Not only were the trails muddy but we often encountered streams where there was no way a vehicle could get across. Sometimes we waded through them and in some cases there was a log on which we could walk across (very carefully). To supplement our water rations we sometimes picked green coconuts, stabbed them with our bayonets and drank the juice. They said it tasted like champagne but you couldn't prove it by me since I had never tasted champagne, but the juice was delicious.

At the end of the first day, we walked down a steep embankment into a beautiful valley with a fast moving stream of very clean water. It was an ideal spot to enjoy a K ration dinner and spend the night. I thought I felt a fever coming on and dreaded the thought if it got worse. However, next morning I felt refreshed and was ready to go.

One disadvantage of this valley was that we had to climb back out of it to the main trail. Tom Rowan carried the machine gun out and it just about did him in. He didn't (or couldn't) carry it the rest of the day. The rest of us chipped in and managed to get to our first destination at the end of the second day of marching. These two days had to be the toughest I had ever spent, before or since. Most of the trails were muddy and our boots and socks were wet from the trails and walking through streams. The highest mountains on Leyte are about 4,400 feet above sea level and I'm sure we encountered the highest.

We were now on an open hill high up in the Leyte Mountains from which on a clear day you could see the Pacific Ocean. There was one Filipino family living on a hut on stilts nearby. We stayed at this location almost a week. On about the third day a second platoon patrol encountered a party of about 5 Japs and killed them all with no casualties. The next day we were alerted that there was movement in the nearby woods. We all took up defensive positions—mine behind the machine gun. I was really scared as we were just one company of men and help was miles away … and we hadn't dug foxholes. What was it in the woods? A pack of wild monkeys!

H Company was ordered to rejoin the Battalion at Burauen, almost a day's march away. We marched in normal order, the 1st, 2nd and 3rd platoons with the first squad of the 1st platoon as the "point". We stopped for a K ration lunch and shortly after resuming the march the scouts came upon a small hill with a single Filipino hut near the top and they thought they saw some movement around it. Sgt. At, our platoon sergeant, briefed me and told me to go to the base of the hill, on the right flank and set up the machine gun. I got to the base of the hill, which had been cleared of all trees, set up the tripod and looked up. I definitely saw movement, near the hut about 40-50 yards away. Tom Rowan handed me the machine gun which I placed in the tripod. I looked up again and sure enough there were several Japs standing around the hut. Jim Kolkman brought up a box of ammo with which I quickly loaded the gun and opened fire. As soon as I fired, the scouts and rifleman at the top of the hill, still well concealed in a wooded area, opened up as well. In the meantime, Sgt. At sent rifleman Sieber to be the machine gun team's right flank protection.

Parenthetically it should be mentioned that mounting and loading the machine gun in training was sometimes monotonous and boring but sure paid off in this case. Unfortunately the machine gun belts were adversely affected by all the damp weather and I couldn't get more than 6 or 8 rounds off before a stoppage occurred. That would require reloading by pulling the bolt back twice. Also the gun was mounted pointing up hill on ground with tree stumps, twigs, weeds and long grass making it difficult to use the sights. Every fifth round was a tracer and that's how I could tell where the rounds were going. The bottom line is that it is unlikely that any of my rounds hit any of the Japs near the huts (although they could have hit some in the woods behind the hut if any were there). Three dead Japs were found when the shooting stopped.

Sieber our right flank protection was shot in the chest during this battle. He lay on the ground seriously wounded. Cap'n Mac now had a tough decision to make. He decided rather than transport Sieber now, he and the 2nd and 3rd platoons would finish the march to rejoin the battalion, then send medical help.

We waited about an hour watching carefully every nook and cranny in the surrounding woods when Lt. Stokely, platoon leader, thought it would be better to rejoin the battalion as soon as possible rather than wait for medical aid, so we gathered up our equipment and moved out.

We thought we were loaded down before but now it was much worse. A litter had been part of the equipment brought into the mountains and now it could be used for the 180 lb. Sieber. It would take four of us to carry it with Sgt. At taking the right rear position with me on the left rear. Dick Ostrom did not carry the machine gun as much as the rest of us because he was a scout but now he had that weapon as well as his rifle.

During this march we noticed no sounds coming from Sieber and no movement of any kind. We stopped to check and sure enough he had passed away. Though this type of event was not totally unexpected it was still a traumatic event for all of us. All we could do was pack up and keep on going which we did, finally reaching the battalion rendezvous point about an hour before dusk.

The other three companies of the 3rd Battalion (Hqtrs 3rd, G and I) had set up a perimeter for the night, so we were allowed to stay inside the perimeter which meant no guard duty that night! What a relief. We dug slit trenches just deep and long enough to sleep in and yet providing adequate cover in case of enemy activity.

The next day we marched to Mahonag where a division hospital was to be established. This march was different from the others because for more than an hour at the end, the trail went up at about a 45 degree angle. We were somewhat surprised but not disappointed that Sgt. At called for a break every 30 minutes or so.

Mahonag was not a town—it was just a large field where all the trees had been cut down. It was to be a major base where food and supplies would be dropped, mostly by single engine "piper cubs" or by twin engine C-47's. Dropping supplies was a hit and miss proposition because in the case of the single engine plane, the pilot not only had to fly the plane but also throw the box out. In one case a crate landed in the temporary hospital killing a patient. Heavier supplies were put in bundles and dropped from C-47's by parachutes. At the temporary hospital setup parachutes were all that stood between the heavens and patients. Tents were dropped later.

As we started out the following morning we realized that the farther we got into the mountains the greater the chance of meeting a strong enemy force. That's exactly what happened. The 3rd Battalion moved out with I company in the lead followed by G with H Company bringing up the rear. This march was very somber. Quiet and eyes to the flanks was the general rule. At one point the warning "watch the right flank", a message which may have been passed back by 300 or more troopers.

I Company came upon the main Japanese supply trail, a wooden corduroy road wide enough for a jeep if a jeep could parachute to use it. No sooner had they discovered the trail when all hell broke loose. Lt. Maloney, platoon leader of the lead platoon, was killed. (He had a B.A. degree in philosophy from Boston College.) The hill where this action occurred was named Maloney Knoll after this battle. I and G Companies continued to move westward while H Company was given the job of holding Maloney Knoll.

The first order of business in this situation, which was pretty much the same all the time after a day's march, was to set up a perimeter by digging foxholes. The general rule was two man foxholes, my partner being the assistant machine gunner Tom Rowan. This perimeter was roughly in circular shape, with the dog-faces on the periphery and the officers and most sergeants on the inside. Once the foxholes were dug and only after they were dug, could one think about a gourmet meal—K rations! Before dark contact was made with the enemy and although there was a lot of firing there were no casualties on our side. As dusk turned to darkness we felt we were ready with the machine guns set up and loaded plus an M1 rifle and a carbine at our fingertips.

High up in the Leyte Mountains on this dark night the Japanese exhibited to us what was really peculiar behavior but to them it was what they considered their psychological weapon: yelling and screaming at the top of their lungs. They were only 20 to 30 yards from us on the north side of our perimeter where our foxhole was located.

To the uninitiated this would appear to be a good spot for a hand grenade to take care of the bad guys. However this was still a jungle setting with trees and underbrush everywhere. Though trees could normally be seen silhouetted against the dark sky, if the grenade was not thrown accurately it could bounce back and have the opposite of the effect intended. Even if the throw was accurate there was no guarantee it would do any damage since the enemy could be heard but even in the daytime was rarely seen. Not that grenades were never thrown—they were—but because each man had only two and resupply was in great jeopardy, they were never thrown indiscriminately.

These nights were <u>long</u> and miserable. The guys in most foxholes settled on a two hours on, two hours off arrangement. Without anything to do except watch for enemy infiltrators it is hard to imagine any other situation where time would pass more slowly. Several times in the early morning hours I perceived that dawn was breaking. Half an hour later there was no dawn! It was a mirage. Finally, after what seemed like a millennium, daylight arrived. Out came the cigarettes and lighters. Some guys chowed down on K rations.

Seeing daylight was like a big load lifted off your shoulders. The long night, often interspersed with rain, was finally over! Sleep during the "2 hour off" period was sometimes very difficult but oftentimes sheer fatigue dictated sleep anyway.

There was a trail along a series of ridges from Maloney Knoll leading to the west side of the island. The other companies of the battalion had continued on this trail and were now about a half mile ahead of us. The third platoon was ordered to go on patrol and make contact with the other companies. They had no sooner started when the lead scout was shot by a sniper. The platoon sergeant went to the scout's aid and he too was shot. Then the platoon leader, 1st Lt. Diffenbaugh, went forward to help and he too was shot by the sniper. Eventually the sniper was killed and the 3 wounded men were evacuated back to Maloney Knoll. There was a doctor with us at that time but he had absolutely no facilities to help the wounded. Unfortunately, neither Sgt. DeLuiga nor Lt. Diffenbaugh survived the night. PFC Swartz, the scout, was eventually evacuated out of the mountains and returned to the states. He survived the war.

The next day the 2nd platoon was sent to contact the other companies. They were successful in their mission however, when they attempted to return to rejoin the rest of H Company on Maloney Knoll, they were stopped by snipers and forced to spend the night with G and I Companies. This put an extra burden on 1st and 3rd platoons back on Maloney Knoll. The section of the perimeter normally occupied by the 2nd platoon had to be divided up between the other two platoons and anybody else available. Our machine gun team was moved from the foxholes we dug facing north to a 2nd platoon foxhole facing east. The foxhole on our left was vacant while the one on the right was occupied by Charlie Doyle, matched with our supply sergeant, John Myers who had spent the previous night inside the perimeter. (He was considered a first class supply sergeant but his infantry skills had not been tested; he was also about 10 years older than the average dogface in our unit.)

Little did we know that this would become a very weird night. A couple hours after dusk a shot rang out from the foxhole to the right of us and Charlie Doyle yelled: "John, you SOB, you shot me." This was a startling and unwelcome development but the unwritten law not to move around at night was strictly adhered to. But questions were raised: How bad was Charlie's wound? Who was Myers shooting at? (Don't ask!) We couldn't get answers until daybreak. A couple hours later shots rang out from <u>within</u> the perimeter. More questions: Did Japs infiltrate the perimeter? Assuming it was a Jap who was shot were there others inside the perimeter? These two incidents occurred before midnight which meant we had to wait about 7 hours before we would have answers. It turned out that a Filipino guerrilla attached to our unit had gotten up and started to move around, apparently unaware of the unwritten law when he was shot and killed by one of our own men.

The second platoon returned the following day without incident. H Company was then ordered to leave Maloney Knoll and rejoin G and I Companies which we did and immediately dug foxholes.

It was about this time that Japanese paratroopers jumped on our air strip from which our supply planes had been taking off. It took a couple days to find and eliminate these "mischief makers." In the meantime we were totally out of food and it wasn't like we were resupplied as soon as the planes started flying again since nearly the entire division had to be supplied and it was still the rainy season. We were without food for about four days.

Dave Renaud and Dick Ostrom, Leyte Island, 1944

Despite these difficulties our main objective was to get to Ormac on the west side of Leyte. To this end H Company, with the 1st squad of the 1st platoon, was given the job of leading the charge. We no sooner had started out when we were stopped by snipers. The 3rd squad of the 1st platoon was the mortar squad and they were ordered to start firing their 60 mm mortar at enemy position. Standard practice was to aim beyond the enemy positions and gradually bring the shells closer to the enemy positions. An upfront observer would give the appropriate instructions and these would be relayed to the mortar squad. When shells started landing near the target, or just beyond, the observer gave an order to back off a given number of yards. Somewhere along the line the order was misinterpreted and the next shell landed close to us. I got hit by a small piece of shrapnel in the right shoulder which caused considerable bleeding. Joe Yarchak, a fellow squad member, used his bayonet to cut off the sleeve of my fatigue jacket so a compress could be applied to the wound. (The shrapnel lodged in my shoulder, eventually migrated to my back and was removed by a local surgeon in 1963, nearly 20 years later!) The battle continued but we were unable to eliminate the snipers so our drive west was stalled.

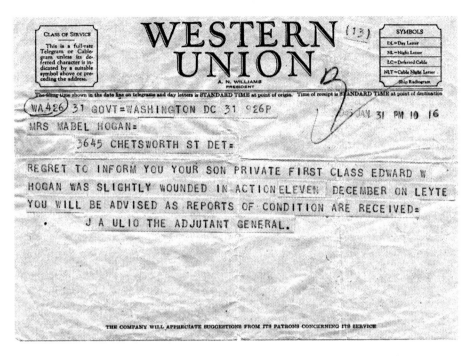

Western Union telegram sent to inform parents of shrapnel wound.

When H Company left Maloney Knoll another company was supposed to occupy the hill but they did not appear at the appointed time so the Japs took advantage and occupied it themselves. Since this was such a strategic spot, the junction of the main foot trail and the Jap supply trail, it was imperative that the hill be retaken. Several unsuccessful attempts were made before, after a few days, B Company did retake the hill.

About this time, probably because of the loss of blood and lack of food, I developed a bad case of dengue fever. I made it back to a temporary hospital in the mountains but was so sick I couldn't even eat. Even after the food supply lines were opened I still couldn't eat. They even dropped ice cream which I didn't want. They told me if I didn't force food down I would never get out of there. Finally I started feeling better, started eating again and was cleared to leave. By this time the 511th had eliminated enemy forces in the area and had made it to the west side of Leyte. I joined a litter party and we headed west. The route took us over Maloney Knoll which was littered with dead Japanese soldiers. The bloating and stench of the bodies was unbearable. By late afternoon of December 24th we came out of the jungle and viewed from a hill, the Pacific Ocean. Behind was almost a month of the most grueling, tense and traumatic events we had ever experienced. To see this ocean, level ground and some of the guys from the outfit was a joy to behold.

On Christmas morning I was hoping for scrambled eggs which most certainly would have been the powdered kind but that didn't matter. To my chagrin the breakfast menu was pancakes so, while a little disappointed, it was still better than what we had been eating. It's just that I wanted something more solid.

I had orders to report to a hospital before rejoining my unit which I did. After a couple days I was discharged and was able to rejoin good old H Company which was now back on the east side of Leyte. H Company Street ran east and west perpendicular to the beach and the western most edge of the Pacific Ocean. Since we were 1st squad of the 1st platoon we had the first tent next to the beach!

Joe Vannier, Editor of I-Company News, gives an account of an incident in Rock Hill, Leyte, which he called "Chappie's Sermon", delivered in December, 1944, in the following:

> It was mid December, 1944, in the rain forest hills of central Leyte, a small island in the Philippines. A group of soldiers were huddled together in small groups in a defensive perimeter atop a mountain, these Troops would name "Rock Hill."
>
> These men had fought and clawed their way across the Leyte Valley from the east, and worked their way up into the Mohan Mountains during the marathon tropical rains of late fall. Surrounded by enemy troops on all sides, they had been without food and medical supplies for nearly a week.
>
> Cut off from the outside world, they might occasionally hear the angry buzzing of a lone reconnaissance plane circling overhead just above the ground fogs and mists that shrouded this mountaintop encampment.
>
> Into this dismal and almost hopeless scene entered Chappie Walker, a young Presbyterian Minister, barely six years out of his seminary training.
>
> Word was passed along to the grimy, unshaven, bleary eyed perimeter Troops that a prayer meeting would be held near the makeshift jungle hospital where the wounded and dying lay shivering on ponchos in the ankle deep mud. It was not far from a small graveyard where the newly dead lay sleeping in shallow mud filled graves.
>
> There, under the gentle guidance of Chappie, these men prayed together. Later, with a few drops of lemon flavored water from a canteen cup and a few crumbs from a k-ration biscuit, Communion was shared.

That day, the skies opened briefly, and a few bundles of food were dropped before the clouds closed in again. It was a mixed blessing, for two Soldiers were killed by the plummeting supply bundles.

A few days later, with strengthened hope and renewed faith, these Troops fought their way through the enemy lines and made their way down a narrow, muddy trail to the shores of the South China Sea.

It was with mixed feelings that they left Rock Hill, for as they led and carried their wounded down the steep slippery slopes, there was an ache in their hearts as they turned briefly for a final look at those rugged handmade crosses atop Rock Hill.

Many would later call this sequence of events "Divine Intervention." And most surely the requirements for "Chappie's Miracle" had been fulfilled.

—From *Alarming Cry News*, Summer, 2003

In general the outfit was in rough shape. Almost everyone had lost weight; some had diarrhea or some other problem. I developed an ear infection which fortunately was cured by medication after one visit with an eye, ear, nose and throat doctor at the army hospital.

6

The big job now was to get the outfit back in fighting shape and fill the holes in the ranks. To that end H Company got about 15 replacements from the states, all paratroopers, but with no combat experience. Our squad leader when we landed on Leyte was an ex-radio man who got promoted, some said, because his dad was an officer in another outfit. In any case, he did not pan out and was replaced by the assistant squad leader, Joe Yarchak. I was named the assistant, another name for which was "captain of the machine gun team" thus gaining 2 stripes from PFC (one stripe) to buck sergeant (3 stripes).

For the most part this was a happy time on Leyte. There were no tough assignments and we were back to eating good old army chow. There was swimming during the day and movies some nights, although it was necessary on occasion to have your poncho and helmet liner on to avoid getting soaked. (Movies of course were outside and so was mass every Sunday.) I remember seeing what I considered a classic, "Rhapsody in Blue" on a rainy night but it was still very enjoyable. We had a Filipino house boy who was named Benny, who did odd jobs for us like filling our canteens, taking the trash out, etc. He was a happy kid, almost always smiling, a pleasure to have around. We lived in pyramidal tents, same as New Guinea, with six men to a tent and slept on cots.

On New Year's Eve 1944, several of us sat on the beach looking out at the vast Pacific Ocean wondering what the new year, 1945, would bring. We had hopes and anxieties but one thing we all agreed on was to get the war over with and get home.

In late January 1945, we boarded trucks for a trip to the airport at Tacloban where C-47 planes awaited us for a relatively short trip to the island of Mindoro. Mindoro is close to Luzon where we were scheduled to make a jump (although we didn't know it yet) in early February. We set up camp near a river that was 75-100 yards wide, 5 feet deep at the deepest point with fast moving clean water.

In some ways life on Mindoro, which was in the middle of the dry season, was easy going and relaxing. However, we did not have our pyramidal tents or cots which meant sleeping on the ground, nor did we have our kitchen crew. For the first time we were introduced to Ten in One rations, a day's meals for ten men. Each large box contained four smaller boxes, so two boxes would to go to five men and the other two going to five others. For breakfast there was a can of bacon, hard biscuits, jam and instant coffee. The boxes were coated with wax so they were used to produce the fire that cooked the bacon and coffee. The wax slowed the burning making it possible to cook everything thoroughly. In general "10 in 1" rations were ample and "relatively" delicious, certainly an improvement over K rations.

My close friend Dick Ostrom, had a buddy in the Air Force who was also stationed on Mindaro. One night Dick and I went over to his base for dinner and what a dinner! We had not seen food like this in some time. Unfortunately I over ate. After dinner we went to where there was a good supply of cold beer, however, since I felt so full, I could hardly drink. Maybe that was a blessing in disguise. In any event the whole evening was a pleasant experience.

On February 3, 1945, early in the morning, we packed up, boarded trucks and went to the hangar where our chutes were stored. (They were packed by riggers.) When we came out of the hangar we were shocked that someone had stolen 2nd Lt. Atkinson's rifle with a scope. (Sgt. At, our old platoon sergeant, had been given a battlefield commission after the fighting on Leyte.) It turned out that this incident was a bad omen. (We assumed that one of the truckers who stayed with his truck when we went into the hangar stole the rifle.)

The trucks took us to the airfields where we climbed aboard C-47's for the relatively short ride to Luzon. This would be our first combat jump but we knew from intelligence sources that there were not many Japs in the area. However since we had only made two jumps in the past 14 months or so we were very rusty and most of us sweated this jump to the max.

The jump went well except that we missed the drop zone by about 3 miles. We were about 30 miles from Manila adjacent to Tagatay Ridge, a sharp angled cliff that must have extended at least 1000 feet down. (If we landed at the base of the ridge we would have had a long climb up!!) Several of us gathered together quickly and set out to find the parachute bundle containing the machine gun, which we did without too much difficulty. (Not finding it would have been a disaster.) We stayed on Tagatay Ridge one more night apparently waiting for the other units of the Division, who landed by ship, to catch up to us. We then moved into the outskirts of Manila. The enemy was very strong in this area. Some of the artillery was of U.S. Navy origin which they acquired when they invaded the Philippines at the beginning of the war.

We were within a mile or two of Nichols Field along the main highway when we were subjected to an artillery barrage which brought our advance to a halt. Most of us took cover in a ditch along side of the highway, and while we were waiting, platoon Sgt. Doug Shorter came by holding his hand over a small but bleeding shrapnel wound to the head. Shorter said: "At has been hit bad." That was certainly bad news but we continued to play the waiting game until a battalion officer came by and asked: "Are there any non-coms here?" I said: "yes." He said, "the outfit has moved out—get going." (A combination of bushes and weeds obscuring our forward vision is the reason we were not aware the troops ahead of us had moved out.)

We got back onto the highway and after walking only a short distance we saw Sgt. At lying on his back covered by a poncho with only his boots sticking out … he died with his boots on. This was one of the worst sights I had seen in the whole war—sending morale down to "ground zero." At had been a tough but fair platoon sergeant and he didn't change the short time since he became a 2nd lieutenant. It was clear he would be sorely missed.

The route to Nichols Field was fraught with peril, mostly from mortar and artillery fire of which we had not seen much in Leyte. Included in the casualties around this time were the Assistant Divisional Commander and our Regimental Commander Col. (The Rock) Haugen, both KIA. Also killed in action were Bernard Denich, assistant machine gunner in our squad and Sgt. Charles Hancock, mortar squad leader in the 1st platoon. Hancock was a fellow Michigander and had been married on his last furlough.

Late one afternoon as we approached Nichols Field, we walked alongside a built up wall of earth about 5 feet high that was either an abandoned railroad or a rice paddy. We could see Japanese solders about 150 yards away on the other side of the built up wall going through some kind of sunset exercise or religious practice. We ignored them because our mission was to recapture Nichols Field.

With all the casualties some changes were necessary, one of which was I was made squad leader of the 1st squad with staff sergeant rank (3 stripes on top, one on the bottom). I was asked if I would take Private Ed Pointkowski as my assistant. He was part of the cadre when the regiment was formed and had been a Sergeant and our first squad leader when we arrived at Camp Toccoa. But before going overseas, while at Camp Polk, his wife came down to visit him. Unfortunately, the order came down: "no weekend passes for anyone." Pointkowski went to town anyway to see her and paid the price—he was busted down to private. I did not get along with him at all and did not want him as my assistant. So I said no to Pointkowski; I wanted Dick Ostrom. Lt. Chas. Stoeckley, our Platoon Leader, and Company Commander Capt. Pat McInnis, (Capt. Mac), agreed.

Dick Ostrom, Lyle Henderson, Ed Hogan (L to R), Luzon, 1945

The last obstacle we encountered before Nichols Field was a stream about 5.5 feet deep and 25 feet wide. There was only one way to get through it and that was to walk through it and of course getting soaked from neck to foot.

One of my first assignments as squad leader was to take a patrol to the rear areas and get rations for the company. About five or six of us went to the rear areas but couldn't find the food storage and nobody we encountered on the way knew either. There was intermittent shell fire in the area (more than where we had just come from) making it risky to stay too long plus darkness was fast approaching. We gave up on finding the food and went back empty handed. It was discouraging after foodless days on rainy, mountainous Leyte to go through the same thing on level, dry Luzon.

We spent the night on a rear area of Nichols Field where a sign still stood that read "U.S. Military Reservation—Keep Off." The Japanese were apparently unaware of the sign's existence.

The next morning the move to retake this valuable air field began. As we waited for the forward elements to move out a shot rang out and I heard a helmet liner hit the ground behind me. I turned around and saw that it belonged to one of the two Filipino guerillas that were attached to our platoon. He had been shot in the head and died instantly. (The other Filipino, who we named Charlie, was invaluable to us as he knew where every Jap employment was.) The one who had just been shot was Charlie's 16 year old nephew, who had been wearing the plastic helmet liner but did not have the steel helmet that went over the liner. It's not likely that the steel helmet would have saved him but it was possible.

This was a tough day for us. The Japs were using 20 and 40 mm anti-aircraft weapons against us. For the most part it was running from one bomb crater to another for cover. Our platoon leader, Lt. Stokely, was killed this day and Joe Yarchak was shot in the upper part of his right leg and that was the end of him as far as fighting in WWII was considered. (He was sent home but recovered.)

Progress was slow but steady. In the afternoon I was in one of the hangars which had been bombed successfully by our planes. Most of the steel pillars were still standing but the roof and sidings had been blown away. I was kneeling on one knee behind a wrecked Jap plane when a bullet hit the front hand guard of my rifle and tore it out of my hands. I immediately got down on my stomach and looked around but could not see any enemies. When we started moving again we came across a litter collection area and there was Joe Yarchak on a stretcher. I asked him if I could have his rifle to replace my damaged one but he said: "No Ed, I may need it." It's true he may have had to pass through some dangerous areas on the way back to the rear even though he would be on a stretcher so his rejection was understandable.

In late afternoon we finally got off Nichols Field, it was now entirely in our hands. It was reported that H Company was down to 61 men from a normal strength of 121. (At a reunion in Washington D.C. in 1990 Capt. Mac said we were actually down to 49 men.) The 2nd platoon was hit hard so the survivors were placed temporarily into the 1st and 3rd platoons.

Before we even got settled in a field behind a wooden fence (excellent for concealment), Charlie announced that he was leaving us temporarily so he could go tell the mother of his nephew about the nephew's untimely death. Then Capt. Mac told me the first squad of the first platoon would be the "point", the squad that would lead in the morning. I was filled with great fear and trepidation. So many casualties already and now we had to attack directly into the face of the enemy. We could see through a hole in the fence that there was an open field about 100 yards long with a small Filipino hut at the far end. If the Japanese were in the hut or hiding at the other end of the field we could be in for trouble. The order of march was first scout Dave Renaud, second scout Lyle Henderson, myself, Dick Ostrom and the machine gun team and finally the remaining riflemen. We were only a few yards from one of the main highways leading into Manila and, just before we were ready to move out, we heard yelling and screaming coming from the highway. What was it but Filipino civilians coming to greet us—the Japanese had retreated deeper into the city. What a relief! After a short wait we started up the highway and after a short distance the highway was lined on both sides with happy civilians with big smiles on their faces. Since we were still the point we were the first troops to liberate this section of Manila and the first to see the genuine happiness of the Filipino people who were fed up with the Japanese occupation. They had fruit and flowers to offer us but the smiles on their faces were enough satisfaction for us.

Detroit News Headline, February 5, 1945

When we reached the northern extremity of the area we were to conquer we stopped and set up camp. (Three other infantry divisions, 1st Cavalry, 37th and 42nd were attacking from the north so a stopping point had been set so that we wouldn't end up shooting at each other.) Our designated area was a city street containing mostly small stores. The second story of one of these buildings was occupied by a dentist who befriended one of our guys, Stu Boze. Some of us were invited to his place for a single shot of American whiskey. It was a very good visit and showed how much we had in common with the Filipino people. In my case I figured Stu Boze owed me one because he was part of the mortar squad that fired its shell, a piece of which ended up in my right shoulder.

We didn't know it at the time, but the worst part of the battle for Luzon was over. There were difficult times ahead but the number of casualties dropped drastically.

7

After a few days at this location in Manila we were ordered to go to Fort McKinley. At the new location we didn't see any buildings—we were set up on a hill with a rolling countryside view. Nothing happened the first couple days but then on the third day 1st Sgt. Jerry Thomas stood up and started to walk up the hill to get his dinner rations when a shot rang out and struck him. He died instantly. This was a tremendous shock to us to have it happen so suddenly. He had to be judged the top recruit who joined the outfit at Camp Toccoa because he was named first sergeant, the highest NCO rank, and the only recruit in H Company to get that rank.

At this point we either set up on the reverse slope of the hill or settled in or close to our fox hole. Nothing else of consequence happened at this location after that.

For the next few weeks we moved from place to place, usually staying a few days at each. It was normal to set up a perimeter and dig foxholes or slit trenches and go on patrols looking for the enemy. On these patrols you had to be very careful and watchful. Usually we would not see any Filipinos—they were gone if there was a chance any Japs were around. This added to the strange silence that pervaded each patrol and tended to reinforce the cautious attitude each of us had.

At one of these locations, our booby trap expert PFC Payne set up hand grenades connected by wire such that if anyone tripped the wire a hand grenade would go off. That night nothing happened so our expert set about removing the booby traps the following morning. Unfortunately he accidentally tripped a wire and a grenade went off, a piece of which hit him in the mid section. It didn't look too bad but a few days after he was taken to an army hospital he died. The really bad thing in this case was that he had three brothers who had already been killed in the war.

After being in action for almost three months, we were told we were going to a rest camp. There were no trucks available but the Army had a solution to that problem: Let them "hoof it." We marched about 12 miles but since it wasn't practical to get to the camp that night they decided we would bivouac along side of the highway and get to the camp the following morning. About 6:00 a.m. the following morning we were awakened and told to get ready to go back to the area we had left the day before. It seems an Army Jeep with a lieutenant and two enlisted men drove up a side road toward a small mountain and were ambushed by Japanese soldiers, who killed the three men and set fire to the Jeep.

Surprise!! Trucks were available to take us back! Our mission was to recover the bodies and the Jeep. It was decided that the 1st squad of the first platoon would be the point. We were in a coconut grove, with another coconut grove about 400 yards in front of us and with absolutely no trees between the two groves. We were told that yesterday afternoon the Japs had a machine nest across the field, in the coconut grove. Our orders: go see if it's still there. We started out in the usual order: 1st scout Dave Renaud, 2nd scout Lyle Henderson, me, the machine gun team, etc. We started out very carefully and slowly. Strangely we thought, we got to the other grove without being fired on. There was a long delay, then finally the order to continue on. Our path so far had been right next to the road the Jeep had traveled the day before. Now that we were in the coconut grove we just followed the road. After about 150 yards the road turned to the right at about a 45 degree angle. There was a group of 6 men that was our left flank protection so when the road turned they turned too. In so doing they started to cross a shallow ravine and lo and behold there were Japs in the ravine. A couple shots were fired, there was some yelling, but nobody was hit. Each of us was able to take cover. The flank protection retreated back to the main body. A decision had to be made now. I thought it best to go back and ask the company commander (Capt. Kitz) what he wanted to do. When I got back there he was in a deep bomb crater and acted like he didn't want to get involved. He thought about calling for a couple tanks. In the end he said pull your men back. I told him "I disagree with your tactics" but that didn't matter to him. I went back and gave hand signals to Dick Ostrom and the 1st platoon pulled back.

There was another long delay and finally the order came to proceed. The Japs had left the ravine, but Dave the lead scout proceeded very slowly and cautiously, wise action considering what had just happened. After a while the brass in the back were getting impatient so they sent G Company on a parallel path to ours but several hundred yards to our right, through an area less likely to contain any Japs. In retrospect I thought of the two long delays they imposed on us which kept us from getting the whole job done and getting it done a lot sooner.

Dick Keith and Ed Hogan holding Japanese flag with rest of squad,
Luzon, 1945

This last event concluded our combat on Luzon and, for that matter, for the war. We set up pyramidal tents in this very area not far from the town of Lepa. This also meant cots—no more sleeping on the ground—for a while anyway. More replacements joined the outfit some of whom had stripes. Dick Ostrom who had been promoted to buck sergeant and was told to put sergeant on his return address mail was now told he wasn't a sergeant after all. Another guy, a sergeant from the states with no combat experience, was now the assistant squad leader in the first squad. It was a devastating blow to Ostrom as well as to the rest of us but with the Army nothing could be done. The Army also decided to beef up all the units, apparently feeling that a 12 man squad was not effective when casualties starting coming in.

8

It was early August, 1945 and with U.S. in control of the Philippines, we settled into a life of training—preparing for the invasion of Japan. On August 6th, one of the guys walking down the company street (a wide dirt path between two rows of tents) announced the news of the first atom bomb that was dropped in Japan. Not long after that a second atom bomb was dropped and a few days later Japan agreed to sign a peace treaty aboard the battleship Missouri. A few days later we were told around mid morning not to leave camp. A couple hours later we were told to pack everything—we were leaving. Around mid-afternoon we were taken to the airfield in trucks and climbed aboard a four engine C-54. The plane was heavily loaded so the pilot asked 6 or 8 of us to stand up front as far as possible (so much for the seat belts). He thought he might have a flat tire so was reluctant to start the take off but he finally realized it was OK to take off. On August 11, we landed safely on Okinawa. Now we just had to wait patiently for the next trip, the final destination, Japan.

Our stay in Okinawa was exemplified by a famous saying attributed to Army practices: "Hurry up and wait," because we ended up staying on this island for almost 2 weeks. Again we were without our pyramidal tents and battalion kitchen. The menu for most meals was Ten in One rations. However, we found we were welcome at most Army and Navy camps that had complete kitchens in operation. Just about every night, Dick Ostrom, two replacements, PFC's Moriarity and Montesanti, and I would hitchhike rides to various bases and enjoy a delicious dinner.

Japan finally surrendered on August 15, 1945 after the dropping of the atom bombs, officially ending World War II. After all details of the surrender were agreed upon we rode trucks to the airport, boarded four engine C-54s and flew to Atsugi Airport, Yokahama. General McArthur flew in with our divisions and was greeted by the 11th Airborne band. He said that was the sweetest music he ever heard. The next day, September 2nd, he and representatives from the Japanese government signed the peace treaty aboard the battleship U.S.S. Missouri.

We spent two or three days in the Yokahama area, then went north to Marioka which was to be our permanent Japanese base. We were quartered in a Japanese grammar school, which turned out to be a reasonably decent place to live.

Once the war ended, the military used a point system to determine eligibility for discharge. Points were earned based on months of service and medals awarded. Having earned the Purple Heart (for being wounded), near the end of October 1945 I had enough points to be eligible for discharge, so I was assigned a seat on a train and headed for a debarkation camp near Tokyo. On November 20, 1945 I boarded the S.S. Sea Sturgeon for the 14 day trip to San Pedro, California. From there we went by train to Fort Sheridan, Illinois where after a couple days I was officially discharged. As part of this process I was given all my back pay and mustering out pay.

S.S. Sea Sturgeon

The last leg of a long journey was the train ride from Chicago to Michigan Central Depot, the point where I started my army career. For some forgettable reason I asked the family not to come to the train station as I wanted to take a cab. After I got off the train I went to where the cabs were and where a relatively large group of people were waiting for a cab. The cabbie master was in charge and he determined who got the next cab. One person would holler "I need a cab to the Statler," another "I need a cab to Dearborn," another "I need one right away to the Book Cadillac." Everyone seemed to be in a hurry but since I had been gone for about 20 months or so I didn't see a need to join the frenzy, so remained silent. Right then the cabbie master came to me and said "Where are you going soldier?" I said, "the East Side." He said, "You get the next cab."

At this time in the U.S. because of shortages of fuel, tires, vehicles, etc. it was standard practice to fill each cab as much as possible. In this case two other parties and I got in the cab and headed for the East Side. (True to the cabbie master's word, it was the next cab that we got into and he'll never know how much that meant to me.) Each party paid their fare when they got to their destination, so when we got to 3645 Chatsworth, the last stop, the cab driver said the fare is $2.50. I gave him a ten dollar bill and told him to keep the change. (I was loaded with my mustering out pay!) He said no and gave me five or six bucks change. He said you'll need it. (He was right!) I rushed into the house where my parents, brothers Dan and Tim, sisters Mary, Barbara, Betty Jo, and Trisha and my aunts Ethel, Zaz (Frances), and Lolly (Pauline) were waiting. It was one happy moment for all, especially me.

As I wrote in my final letter from Japan to my parents: Il est fini! ... an attempt in my limited French to give them an important message—after almost 3 years, the long wait was finally over.

978-0-595-42904-2
0-595-42904-1

Printed in the United States
78352LV00005B/244-315